THE PINEAL GLAND: THE EYE OF GOD

Comprising Chapter XVI of Manly Hall's

Man: The Grand Symbol of the Mysteries

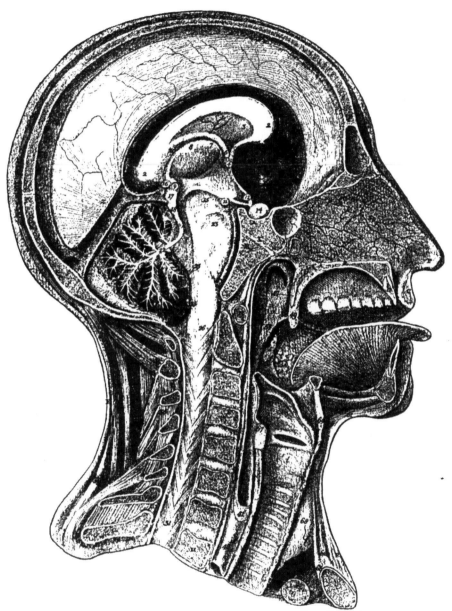

—From Fyfe's Anatomy.

CROSS-SECTION OF THE HUMAN HEAD

*In this figure the corpus callosum is marked (2), the septum lucidum (3), the pituitary
body (14), the pineal gland (16), and the quadrigeminal bodies (17) and (18).
(See page 144 for further details.)*

THE PINEAL GLAND: THE EYE OF GOD

Comprising Chapter XVI of Manly Hall's

Man: *The Grand Symbol of the Mysteries*

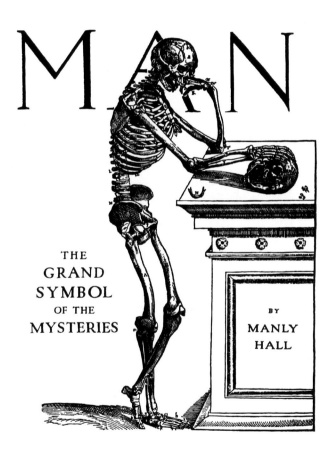

Martino Publishing
Mansfield Centre, CT
2015

Martino Publishing
P.O. Box 373,
Mansfield Centre, CT 06250 USA

ISBN 978-1-61427-845-0

© *2015 Martino Publishing*

Cover design by T. Matarazzo

Printed in the United States of America On 100% Acid-Free Paper

MAN

THE GRAND SYMBOL OF THE MYSTERIES

BY

MANLY HALL

Published by

MANLY P. HALL PUBLICATIONS
LOS ANGELES
1932

THE PINEAL GLAND: THE EYE OF GOD

CHAPTER XVI

THE PINEAL GLAND, THE EYE OF THE GODS

S THE pineal gland was the one most recognized and written about by the earlier adepts, it is the logical beginning of any occult discussion of the endocrine chain. The *epiphysis cerebri*, or pineal body, secures its name from its peculiar shape (the *pinus*, or pine cone) and arises in the fifth week of the human embryo as a blind sac branching off from that section of the brain which is next in front of the mid-brain—the diencephalon—which includes the area of the third ventricle and adjacent parts. The distal, or remote, portion of this sac becomes the body of the gland. The proximal portion (the point of attachment or origin) remains as the stalk. Is not this pine cone the one to which E. A. Wallis-Budge refers in his OSIRIS AND THE EGYPTIAN RESURRECTION, when in describing the entry of Ani into the presence of Osiris in the Egyptian ritual of *Coming Forth by Day* as "the so-called 'cone' on Ani's wig," for which the good Egyptologist could find no intelligent reason? Is this not also the whirring cone which was among the symbolic playthings of the child Bacchus and which Bastius describes as a small cone-shaped piece of wood around which a cord was wound so that it might be made to spin and give out a "humming noise"? (See ORPHEUS, by G. R. S. Mead.) Those acquainted with the esoteric function of the pineal gland or who have experienced the "whirring" sound attendant upon its activity will realize how apt is the analogy.

Ingrowths of connective tissue from the *pia mater,* that delicate and highly vascular membrane investing the brain and spinal cord, later divide the body of the gland into lobules. At birth the structure is comparatively large and by twelve years it has attained its full size. Here again is a possible analogy to the Bacchus myth, for the toy cone was a symbol peculiar to the childhood of the god. In other words, under normal conditions, the gland deteriorates with adolescence. Retrograde evolution, or degeneration, of the pineal body begins about the sixth or seventh year and is practically complete by puberty. It should be distinctly remembered, however, that whereas Nature has eliminated other organs and parts of the primitive man, this has remained; and realizing Nature's economy, we must recognize the gland as still contributing in some way to human functioning. According to Dr. J. F. Gudernatsch, formerly of Cornell University Medical College, "several, at least three, dorsal diverticula *(epiphyses)* develop during the second month of fetal life from the roof of the diencephalon. They are entirely rudimentary in man. The *epiphyses proper* is the most posterior one and is the only one, which, in man, differentiates to any extent. The other two are the *paraphysis* and the *parietal eye,* a rudimentary sense-organ of some reptiles." According to Haeckel, true eyes

1

that cannot see are to be found in certain animals, deeply placed within the head, covered by thick skins and muscles.

The *thyrsus,* or sceptre of the Greek Mysteries, consisted of a staff surmounted by a pine cone and twisted about with grape and ivy leaves. The whole form of this sceptre is symbolic of the spinal cord, its Nadis and plexuses, the pineal gland, and the pneumogastric nerve, all closely related to the mysteries of regeneration. The pineal gland is described by Santee as "a cone-shaped body *(corpus pineale)* 6 mm. (0.25 in.) high and 4 mm. (0.17 in.) in diameter, joined to the roof of the third ventricle by a flattened stalk, the habenula. . . . The pineal body is situated in the floor of the transverse fissure of the cerebrum, directly below the splenium of the corpus callosum, and rests between the superior colliculi of the quadrigeminal bodies on the posterior surface of the mid-brain. It is closely invested by pia mater. The interior of the pineal body is made up of closed follicles surrounded by ingrowths of connective tissue. The follicles are filled with epithelial cells mixed with calcareous matter, the brain-sand *(acervulus cerebri).* Calcareous deposits are found also on the pineal stalk and along the chorioid plexuses. The function of the pineal body is unknown. . . . In reptiles there are two pineal bodies, an anterior and a posterior, of which the posterior remains undeveloped, but the anterior forms a rudimentary, cyclopean eye. In the Hatteria, a New Zealand lizard, it projects through the parietal foramen and presents an imperfect lens and retina and, in its long stalk, nerve fibers. The human pineal body is probably homologous with the posterior pineal body of reptiles."

The *Branchiostoma lanceolatum,* a small transparent marine animal, about two inches in length, is the only vertebrate, so far as known, which does not possess a pineal gland. In reptiles, according to Spencer, the gland is of considerable length and passes out (as noted by Santee) through an opening in the roof of the skull. In the chameleon, the gland lies under a transparent scale in the parietal foramen, and its cordlike middle structure, according to Hertwig, "bears a certain resemblance to the embryonic optic nerve. . . . Investigators who, like Rabl-Ruckhard, Ahlborn, Spencer, and others, have studied the pineal gland, are of of the opinion that *the pineal body must be considered as an unpaired parietal eye, which in many cases, for example in reptiles, appears to be tolerably well preserved, but in most vertebrates is in process of degeneration."* This learned author then affirms the probability that in reptiles the pineal gland reacts to the influence of light, but to what degree must remain *undecided.*

In his lecture on the eyes delivered at the Mayo Clinic and afterwards published by the American Optical Company, Thomas Hall Shastid, A.M., M.D., F.A.C.S., LL.D., etc., said: "Some of the amphibians had a median, or pineal, eye; an eye in the back of the head. Many of the gigantic saurians, too, of the Mesozoic time had this eye, and, in any geological museum, you can still see, in the back of the giant lizard's skull, the hole through which this strange eye formerly looked out. In ourselves the hole has boned over, and the eye has shrunk up into the so-called pineal gland. . . . The pineal eye made its first appearance in the world far back among the invertebrates. It was, indeed, an invertebrate eye (that is, one with the rods turned toward the vitreous, instead of away from it, consequently with no blind spot) but it persisted (still in the invertebrate form of eye) through some of the fishes. through the amphibians generally, through the lizards, and then began degenerating; possibly because the vertebrates had other eyes, and these were of the vertebrate (for some unguessable reason a more suitable) type." Is the occultist, then, unreasonable when he affirms that in the beginning of life upon this

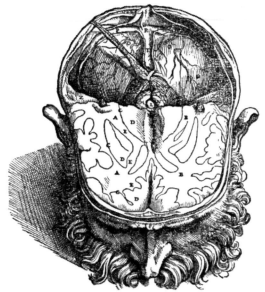

—From De Humani Corporis Fabrica.

THE PINEAL GLAND. (After Vesalius)

planet vertebrates were hermaphrodites and "objectively one-eyed"? Is it not also more reasonable to agree with occultism that this gland actually extended through the skull somewhat like an antenna as an organism of generalized sense perception than to accept the suggestions of Professor Lankester that man was originally transparent so that the inner eye could see through the walls of the head? Did the Egyptians know that reptiles present the highest development of this gland and for this reason coiled the serpent upon their foreheads where the third eye of the Orientals is placed by symbolic license? Was not the uræus the symbol of wisdom and is not the pineal gland the organ of a method of acquiring knowledge which is no longer employed in general but is a secret preserved by the elect?

As an emblem of divinity, the pineal gland would naturally be associated with royalty, for the kings were the shadows of the gods upon earth. The crown of Lower Egypt and also the *Pschent*, or crown of the Double Empire (consolidated Egypt) were surmounted by a curious antenna, feeler, or very thin curved horn, which is most reminiscent of the descriptions of the structure of the third eye that have descended from the first ages. The *Maat*, or ostrich plume of the Law—another Egyptian symbol of truth, is quite similar to the pineal gland in shape and was worn like the feather of the American Indians as though rising from the parietal foramen. By many tribes birds are regarded as emissaries between the manidos and mankind and bird feathers worn in this fashion could easily have a double significance. The peacock feather, with its ocellated spot, is attached to the head of the Chinese mandarin in a position somewhat similar to the pineal gland in the human head (lying backward), and as a symbol of dignity or an enlightened condition accompanying greatness may have a similar origin.

In occultism the pineal gland is regarded as a link between the objective and subjective states of consciousness; or, in exoteric terminology, the visible and invisible worlds of Nature. In the religions of the Latins it was, therefore, referred to as Janus, the two-faced god and keeper of the gates of sanctuary. This divinity was the antitype of St. Peter, who succeeded him as the warder of the heavenly portals and who carries the two keys of his office—one to the golden mystery of the spirit and the other to the silver mystery of the body. Two-faced gods are frequently spoken of in ancient records. Hermae like the *bifrons* Janus may still be seen in old Roman villas, with the occasional and intriguing exception that one of the faces will be male and the other female—the *herm-aphroditus* again? The female face represents the animal soul and the male the divine soul, and the whole figure is indicative of the occult structure and function of the pineal gland. Gould, in his MYTHICAL MONSTERS, gives several examples drawn from the earliest writings of the Chinese. Hindu mythology also abounds in polycephalous divinities, and from the far-off Tibetans we learn that one of the titles of Avalokiteshvara is *Samanta-mukha*, "he whose face looks every way." There is an alchemical mystery also in connection with the pineal gland, for the regeneration of man is dependent upon the tincturing of this gland, which must be transmuted from base metal into gold. Unawakened by Kundalini, the pineal gland is the vehicle of *kama-manas*—the animal mind (Aphrodite)—but when tinctured by the spiritual light, it becomes *buddhi-manas*—the divine mind (Hermes). This buddhi-manas is the Thoth of the later Egyptian Mysteries, the god of learning and letters, and (according to the extravagant statements of his priests) the source of twenty-six thousand books.

The philosophers know that the pineal gland was an organ of conscious vision long before the physical eyes *issued from the brain*, not necessarily or exclusively of such vision as we have today but rather vision of that world wherein man dwelt before his lapse into his present state. As his contact with the physical world grew more complete, the individual lost his functions upon the inner planes of life, together with his conscious connection with the

Creative Hierarchies in the universe about him. Only through discipline—effort directed by wisdom and law—can he rise again into the sphere of his spiritual completeness. It is a mistake to infer that the pineal gland *as a physical body* literally possesses all the occult virtues ascribed to it by the sages. The gland itself is not the third eye, but only the reflection of that organ—its counterpart or symbol in the material constitution. It is a relic bearing witness to an ancient faculty, and because it has endured through these eras of spiritual obscuration, promises the ultimate restoration of the function to which it bears witness. The true power of the gland is in its spiritual counterpart, even as the whole strength of man abides in his invisible nature. The true third eye cannot be seen by the ordinary vision, but is visible to the clairvoyant as a vibrant spectromatic aura surrounding the outer body of the gland and pulsating with an electrical light. "The special physical organ of perception in the brain," writes H. P. Blavatsky, "is located in the aura of the pineal gland. This aura answers in vibration to any impression, but it can only be sensed, not perceived, in the living man. During the process of thought, manifesting in consciousness, a constant vibration occurs in the light of this aura, and a clairvoyant looking at the brain of a living man may almost count, see with the spiritual eye, the seven scales, the seven shades of light, passing from the dullest to the brightest. You touch your hand; before you touch it the vibration is already in the aura of the pineal gland, and has its own shade of color. It is this aura which causes the wear and tear of the organ, by the vibrations it sets up. The brain set vibrating conveys the vibrations to the spinal cord and so to the rest of the body. Powerful vibrations of joy or sorrow may thus kill. The fires are always playing around the pineal gland but when the Kundalini illuminates them for a brief instant the whole universe is seen. Even in deep sleep the third eye opens. This is good for Manas, who profits by it, though we ourselves do not remember."

It was Descartes who saw the pineal gland as the abode of the soul or the sidereal spirit in man. He reasoned that although the *anima* was joined to every organ of the body, there must be one special part through which the divine portion exercised its functions more directly than through the rest. After concluding that neither the heart nor the brain could be as a whole that special locality, he decided through a process of elimination that it must be that little gland which, though bound to the brain, yet had an action or motion independent of it. Descartes concluded that the pineal gland could be put into a kind of swinging motion by the animal spirits which move through the concavities of the skull. We must consider him, therefore, as a powerful figure in the transition period between mediæval and modern science.

We cannot do better than to insert at this point, in Descartes' own words, the arguments by which he convinced himself that the pineal gland was the seat of the soul. The following is extracted from a very early edition of his celebrated treatise, OF MAN, and the terminology is preserved in all the quaintness of the original. "Yet is not the whole Brain the Seat of this Inward

Sense, but only some part of it; for otherwise the Optick Nerves, and the Pith of the Backbone, as being of the same substance with the Brain, would be the Residence of the Inward Sense. Now this peculiar place of the Soul's Residence is the Conarion, or Glandula Pinealis, a certain Kernel, resembling a pine-apple, placed in the midst of the Ventricles of the Brain, and surrounded with the arteries of the Plexus Chorides. The reason why we take this Kernel to be the peculiar Seat of the Soul, is because this part of the Brain is single, and one only. For whereas all the Organs of the Senses are double; there can be no Reason again, why we should not perceive two Objects instead of one; but only because above these Impressions are transmitted to a certain part of the Brain, which is single and one only, wherein both are conjoyn'd. Furthermore, it is also requisite that the part should be movable, to the end that the Soul by agitating of it immediately, might be able to send the Animal Spirits into some certain Muscles, rather than into others. And foreasmuch as this Kernel is only supported by very small Arteries that encompass it, it is certain that the least thing will put it into motion. And therefore we conclude, that this inmost part of the Brain is the Seat of the Soul, in which it exerts its operations of Understanding and Willing of whatsoever proceeds from the Body, or tends towards it."

In ascribing motion to the pineal gland, Descartes, though not an occultist, hit upon one of the most profound secrets of the ancient Mysteries. The great Descartes continues: "Accordingly the Common Sense may be described to be an Internal Sense, whereby all the Objects of the External Senses are perceived and united in the midst of the Brain, as the common Center of all Impressions. Or the Common Sense is nothing else, but the concurrence of all motions made by the Objects upon the Nerves, in the Conarion, happening at the same time that the Objects move the Senses. Neither doth the Smallness of this Kernel hinder its being the Instrument of the Common Sense; but on the contrary, those Persons are the most stupid in whom this Kernel, because of its bigness, is not so easily moved; and those the most witty and apprehensive in whom this Kernel is less, because it is so much the more easily moved: And tho' it were much less than it is, yet would it be big enough with respect to the several Points of the Ventricles, and to the Pipes of the Nerves." For centuries Descartes was ridiculed by the learned, and his mystical conclusions were of that type relegated by the great Tyndall to the field of "poesy." And now at this late day comes a "conditional" vindication of Descartes' views from a science which, all too often, suffers from an "infallibility" complex. "Recently, however, the great Frenchman's idea is gaining favor in the eye of science—that is, if we regard the soul as a department of the human intellect. [Sic!] For, apparently, the pineal gland is concerned directly, although still mysteriously, with the development of intelligence." (See HOW WE BECAME PERSONALITIES.)

Very small children but recently removed from their embryonic recapitulation of humanity's earlier struggle for existence have an extremely sensitive area about the crown of the head where the skull has not yet closed. In rare cases it never closes at all, although usually the sutures unite between the seventh and ninth years. The sensitivity of the area of the head over the third eye during childhood is usually accompanied by a phase of clairvoyance or, at least, sensitiveness. The child is still living largely in the invisible worlds and, while its physical organism is still more or less unresponsive due to its incomplete state, the child has at least a shadow of activity in those worlds with which it was once fully connected through the open gateway of the pineal gland. As the higher intellect—the *Ego* of the Latins—gradually retires into

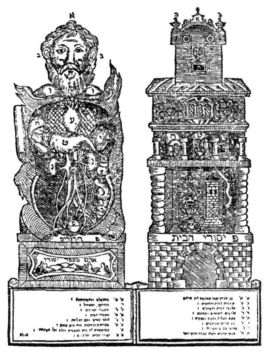

—From Cohn's Treatise on Cabalistical Medicine.

AN EARLY FIGURE SHOWING CORRESPONDENCES BETWEEN THE COM-PARTMENTS OF THE HUMAN BODY AND THE ROOMS OF A HOUSE

the evolving physical structure, it closes the heavenly door behind it. This entry of man into his body is associated in some mysterious way with the "soul crystals" (acervulus cerebri) which form in the pineal gland.

The mystery of the third eye is very beautifully elucidated in the Scandinavian Mystery legends of the World Tree already referred to. In the Eddic tradition it is written that upon the topmost branch of Yggdrasil sat an eagle gazing out upon the universe and upon the head of the eagle, between his eyes, perched a hawk. The eagle has generally been interpreted to signify the element of air and the hawk the ether of space. But when we remember that to the Egyptians the hawk was the peculiar symbol of Horus—whose single eye unquestionably represented the pineal gland to the initiates of his order—the curious figure takes on new importance. A learned Cabalist of the last century declared that from his study of THE ZOHAR and the relation of the Tree of the Sephiroth to the human body, the first Sephira—Kether, the Crown —signified the pineal gland; and that the next two Sephiroth—Chochma and Binah, one placed on either side of it—were the two lobes of the cerebrum. Several statements appear in the Hebrew Scriptures that may be taken as indirect allusions to the pineal gland.

This little body has a tiny finger-like protuberance at one end—that farthest from the point of attachment. This protuberance is called the staff of God and corresponds to the holy spear in the Grail Mysteries. The whole gland is shaped like the evaporating vessels or retorts of the alchemists. The vibrating finger on the end of this gland is the rod of Jesse and the sceptre of the high priest. Certain exercises prescribed in the inner schools of Eastern and Western occultism, when performed by one qualified for such action, cause this finger to vibrate at an incalculable rate of speed, which results in the buzzing or droning sound in the head already mentioned. This phenomenon can be very distressing and may even have disastrous results when brought about without sufficient knowledge of occult matters. The pineal gland and the pituitary body have been called the head and the tail respectively of the Dragon of Wisdom. The psychical and occult currents moving in the brain in their ascent through the spinal cord (see chapter on *Kundalini and the Sympathetic Nervous System)* must pass through the cerebral aqueduct which is closed by the trap door of the pineal gland. When this body—the ibis of the Egyptians—"lies backwards" as it were on its haunches, it closes the opening into the fourth ventricle and forms a sort of stopper. It thus seals in the contents of the third ventricle, dividing them from the fourth. When stimulated by Kundalini, the gland stands upright, lifting itself like the head of a cobra ready to strike and, like the head of this snake, the gland increases in size and its little finger-like protuberance moves with the rapidity of a serpent's tongue. The pineal gland, having removed itself as an obstruction to the passage between the ventricles, permits the essences in the brain to mingle in a spiritual alchemy.

The "All-Seeing Eye" of the Masonic Brethren; the "Eye Single" of the Scriptures by which the body is filled with light; the "One Eye" of Odin which enabled him to know all the Mysteries; the "Eye of Horus" which at one time Typhon swallows up; the "Eye of the Lord" which, as Boehme says, "beholds all"—all these, then, are but allusions to that primitive organ which, according to the commentaries forming the basis of THE SECRET DOCTRINE, "getting gradually petrified," disappeared from view, having been drawn "deeply into the head" and buried "deeply under the hair." It is of this, then, that Proclus writes in his first book ON THE THEOLOGY OF PLATO, where he declares that the soul, having entered into the adytum, or inner recesses of her nature, perceives "the genus of the gods, and the unities of things" without the aid of her objective eyes, which are described as "closed." Is there anything unscientific, then, in affirming that the pineal gland is the third eye of the historico-mythological "men of ancient times," such as are recorded by Berossus in his fragments on the origins of the Chaldeans and of which the Greeks have record in their fables of the Cyclops? The mystic knows that the pineal gland is all that remains of the "Eye of Dangma," the inner eye of the illumined sage, the "Eye of Shiva" placed vertically upon the foreheads of the gods and Dhyanas to signify that in them the spiritual sight is not obscured. When gazing at the inscrutable face of Avalokiteshvara, be reminded by his third eye of the commentaries wherein it is written that when the inner "man" is active, the eye "swells and expands," and the Arhat is able to feel and see this activity and regulate his actions accordingly.